# flourish

## 4 HABITS OF VIBRANT FAITH

TERI LYNNE UNDERWOOD

Scripture quotations marked CSB have been taken from the Christian
Standard Bible®, Copyright ©2017 by Holman Bible Publishers. Used
by permission. Christian Standard Bible® and CSB® are federally
registered trademarks of Holman Bible Publishers.

ISBN: 9798610022185

Cover Image: Lightstock

For all the women who have inspired me to flourish, who have lived out vibrant faith, and who have challenged me to live wholly and whole-heartedly for the Lord.

# DIG IN

We are about to embark on a fun journey together. It's one that began for me in Magdala. Yes, that Magdala, as in Mary Magdalene.

In 2019 Scott and I had the opportunity to spend ten days in the Holy Land. To say it was life-changing doesn't begin to cover it.

The highlight of the trip for me was the opportunity to share with our group of about forty while we were at the gorgeous Magdala Center. (You definitely want to check it out at www.Magdala..org.)

As I prepared for the trip and considered what I would share, I wanted to emphasize the lessons we can learn from the women in Scripture, specifically in the New Testament.

I made a list of all the women named in the books of the New Testament, either by name or with a specific description (like the woman with the issue of blood).

After compiling my list of names, I looked at how they were described, what their interactions with others were, etc. From that, I identified four key areas—four habits—that stood out.

Over the next four weeks, I hope you'll enjoy this journey of digging into each of these areas. And, my prayer is that you'll begin to see how you can nurture each of them.

There is no "one-size-fits-all" method for developing these practices. Rather than outlining specific steps you can take, this study will invite you to consider the heart of each one of the habits and, from that, develop your path to flourishing faith.

Each week you'll have the opportunity to

- Spend time in Scripture, exploring what God's Word reveals about the motivation for each habit;
- Discover women in both the gospels and the epistles who modeled each one;
- And consider what you can do to grow in each area during your current season of life.

## 3 Rs STUDY METHOD

The 3 Rs study method a simple way to work through a portion of Scripture. Each day we'll use this easy three-prong process to observe, interpret, and apply what we read.

Whether you've been doing Bible study for decades or this is your first time, the 3 Rs will help you answer key questions and dig into each day's reading.

## Read (Observation)

The main question we want to consider in this stage is: **What does the passage say?**

- Slowly read through the verses a few times. It may also be useful to read the verses aloud or listen to a Bible app.
- Make note of words or ideas that stand out, are repeated, or you are unclear about.
- Using a regular English dictionary, look up any words that are unfamiliar or you want to make sure you know the meaning of.
- Identify the author, original audience, and context of the passage.

## Reflect (Interpretation)

In this stage of study, we are examining this question: **What does the passage mean?**

- Identify what this passage would have meant to the original audience.
- Look up any cross references or related passages and note how they connect.
- Make a list of what the passage reveals about the character and nature of God.

- Write down what you observe about the character and nature of man.
- Identify the main idea or focus of the verses.
- Write out a short summary of passage.
- Choose a key word or phrase to help you remember what you have read.

Respond (Application)
This is final stage of our study and we are looking at the application question: **How should this passage change me?**

- As you respond to what you have read, it is helpful to consider these three questions: What does this passage teach me about the character and nature of God? How does this understanding of God change my view of myself? What do I need to do to align myself with the revealed truth?
- Considering your list of what you learned about God and what you learned about humanity, identify with specificity what you need to change in order to align yourself with the revealed Word and will of God.
- Pray for wisdom and understanding to apply what you have gleaned in your life.

In addition, each week will offer you opportunities for additional reading and study about each practice.

Are you ready to get started?

# FLOURISH

(n) grow or develop in a healthy or vigorous way

In 2018 we moved onto the property that had belonged to my husband Scott's grandparents. We spent several months gutting the old house and we were excited to be settled into the place we call "Underwood Estates."

I spent a lot of time that first year wandering around our three-ish acres, noticing all the plants and flowers happily growing beside the house, near the fence line, and out near the barn. From the black, clover-looking grass near Scott's workshop to the gardenias along the shed, I wondered how all this flora would fare under my care.

Scott's grandmother, Mamaw Underwood, had a very green thumb. She could root and grow anything. And I was pretty sure those same genes did not run through my family—or least they didn't make into my blood.

Nonetheless, I scoured the internet, looking up the best time to prune the rosebushes and cut back the camellia. I researched what sorts of plants would do well in various places in the yard and even managed to grow some tomatoes in the small raised bed next to our screened porch.

But the truth is, nothing seemed to be flourishing like it had under Mamaw's care.

I had to learn how much water and what sort of food each plant needed, I discovered it really does matter where you put pots of flowers. Plus, those guidelines on the tags about how much sun they need are important to read.

I am definitely not a horticulturalist so I've simplified the growth cycle to the four main aspects I've discovered of raising plants that flourish.

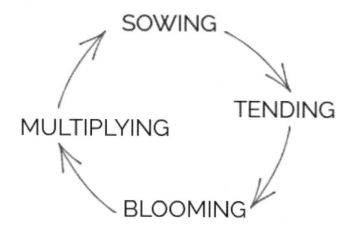

SOWING

TENDING

BLOOMING

MULTIPLYING

And, somewhere along the way, I began to understand why this metaphor of growth is used within Scripture. We're all in some season of the natural growth cycle.

How does this work? What do these stages look like in our spiritual lives?

## Sowing
Maybe you're in a season where you are building a foundation for your faith. This isn't about being a new believer necessarily. It's more about identifying specific areas where you would like to see growth and homing in on the "seeds" you need to plant in order for that to happen.

## Tending
The tending season for my flowers is mostly about making sure I water correctly and feed consistently. Spiritually, tending can look like developing habits that enable growth. Again, there is no one right answer. Just like my gardenias need something different than my day lilies, each one of us is going to tend our spiritual lives in different ways.

## Blooming
This is where we all want to be, right? We want to see blooms. Here the tending becomes visible. We like seeing results, evidence. And, the truth is, we should see those blooms. The fruit of our faith is evidence of God's work in us and it brings Him glory (John 15:8).

The final stage can be the hardest.

## Multiplying

When we think of spiritual multiplication, we often focus on sharing the gospel. But, there's more to consider. When we are multiplying, we are both sowing seeds in ourselves and in others. We are "leveling up" in our own spiritual practices.

*So, Teri Lynne, what does all this look like in real life?* I know, you're wondering. And if you are at all like me, you appreciate an example that spells it out.

Let's consider the practice of Scripture memorization and how it can relate to these four stages.

We start with the realization that we want to memorize Scripture. Maybe we've been challenged by a sermon or inspired by someone else's ability to recite passages. No matter where the inclination begins, the seed is planted. And we sow into that desire.

We tend that new interest by determining what we want to memorize. From there we choose specific methods we will utilize to embed those words in our hearts. For example, I might find an app designed to help or buy index cards to write the verse on and carry with me. We spend time each day learning and reviewing the verse or passage.

Finally, we bloom. We know the verse. We could recite it at any point. And, we tell others about the joy we've discovered in memorizing Scripture. They can observe that something has changed in us.

Because they can see it and because we're excited about it, we move into the multiplication stage. We're encouraging others to consider memorizing Scripture. We're sharing how it's blessed and benefitted us. And, we're enthusiastic about continuing this practice and thinking about what the next verse or passage we memorize will be.

An important reminder
I want to add a little note here because there's something else we need to know about the way this growth cycle can work.

My flowers and small vegetable garden were thriving last year. Until the first week in August. That's the week we went on vacation. And even though I had someone else who graciously came to water my plants, they just didn't thrive.

We got home from our trip and nothing looked as good as it had before we left. Our circumstances had an impact on the growth of my plants.

And, friend, sometimes the circumstances in our lives can adversely affect our spiritual practices and growth.

When that happens, because it will, I want to encourage you not to give up. Your habits and practices may ebb and flow throughout the seasons of your life. The way you do things may shift based on your circumstances or commitments.

Please, please, please, don't think that means you're dying on the vine! I tell people this all the time and I want you to hear it (well, read it):

## God is not interested in your list of accomplishments or giving gold stars for all the things you've done — He is interested in YOU.

He wants to spend time with you. Our goal is to abide in Him so that we can flourish in Him. And that can look different for every one of us in every season of life.

As you move through this study, I hope you will remember that these practices are tools not the goal. Our aim is to be like Jesus, to know Him, and to walk confidently in the knowledge we are accepted and loved by the God of all creation.

serving

# SERVING

serving (v.) — perform duties or services for
(another person or an organization)

We have a tendency to believe serving is
about what we do. We ask ourselves
questions like: *Should I serve in the nursery at
church? Will I help with the food for a grieving
family? What can I do during the holidays to
give back to my community?*

And these are good questions. But when we
focus on what we will do rather than the heart
behind our service, we miss the real point:

## We serve for God's glory, not our own.

Read that again—We serve for God's glory, not
our own.

Before you begin your personal study time this
week, let's explore three truths Scripture
teaches us about serving. Having these
concepts firmly in place will help us as we dig
into the verses over the next few days.

<u>Serving others is evidence of the transforming
work of Christ in us.</u>
We serve because God has changed us. Our
service is an overflow of His work in us. As we
consider the *ways* we will serve, we must first
identify the *whys* we will serve.

Jesus spoke to his disciples concerning this topic in Matthew 20. We'll be looking at those verses in-depth this week, but for now, let's think about reasons why we might want to serve.

Take a moment to write down four or five motives behind serving.

It's vital that we ask the Holy Spirit to help us identify our own reasons for the ways we serve and support others. The disciples wanted power, but Jesus cautioned them not to seek the things of this world.

Why do you serve?

Spend some time in prayer before you begin your study time asking the Lord to reveal your heart in this area and move you to a place of serving out of gratitude for the transformation He has done in your life.

<u>Serving others is an act of submission to the Lord.</u>
I don't know about you, but there have been days in my life when I felt like I was the only one in my house who could see the dirty dishes and unfolded laundry.

A few years ago, I had a particularly bad attitude about that sort of thing and was complaining to a friend. She wisely and gently reminded me to look at those mundane (and sometimes frustrating) tasks as opportunities to submit the Lord by serving the people He placed in my life.

Service isn't usually glamorous, in fact, it can often go unnoticed. But it is a way to submit our own desires and self-focus to the Lord.

Twice in Colossians 3 Paul reminds us about how to view our daily tasks:

And whatever you do, in word or in deed, do everything in the name of the Lord Jesus, giving thanks to God the Father through him. (v. 17)

Whatever you do, do it from the heart, as something done for the Lord and not for people. (v. 23)

Whatever you do, do it in His name and for His sake.

Serving is always rooted in sacrifice.
This theme of sacrifice runs through all of Scripture. It's a topic the Lord wants us to explore and understand. And He wants us to live it out. We are called to sacrificial living. It's not optional.

When we think about sacrifice, we often think about finances (and we'll definitely get to that when we consider the habit of giving). But if we're really honest, sometimes it's a whole lot easier to write a check than it is to give up our time or our preferences.

In Philippians 2, Paul gives us a challenging word:

Do nothing out of selfish ambition or conceit, but in humility consider others as more important than yourselves. Everyone should look out not only for his own interests, but also for the interests of others. (vv. 3-4)

Serving others is often the sacrifice of our own interests. And that is often the most difficult sacrifice we make.

But remember this: our service is a sacrifice that pleases God. It brings Him pleasure and points others toward Him.

**We serve for God's glory, not our own.**

As you spend time reading and looking at Scripture this week, I hope you will keep that truth in focus.

WE SERVE
FOR
GOD'S GLORY
NOT
OUR
OWN.

# DAY 1 — TRUE GREATNESS
## Matthew 20:20-28

READ — KEY QUESTION: What does this passage say?

REFLECT — KEY QUESTION: What does this passage mean?

RESPOND — KEY QUESTION: How should this change me?

What does this passage teach me about the character and nature of God?

How does this understanding of God change my view of myself?

What do I need to do to align myself with the revealed truth?

# DAY 2 — WHY DO WE SERVE?
## 1 John 4:7-11

READ — KEY QUESTION: What does this passage say?

REFLECT — KEY QUESTION: What does this passage mean?

RESPOND — KEY QUESTION: How should this change me?

What does this passage teach me about the character and nature of God?

How does this understanding of God change my view of myself?

What do I need to do to align myself with the revealed truth?

# DAY 3 — FREEDOM TO SERVE
## Galatians 5:12-15

READ — KEY QUESTION: What does this
passage say?

REFLECT — KEY QUESTION: What does this
passage mean?

RESPOND — KEY QUESTION: How should this change me?

What does this passage teach me about the character and nature of God?

How does this understanding of God change my view of myself?

What do I need to do to align myself with the revealed truth?

# DAY 4 — WOMEN WHO SERVED IN THE GOSPELS
## Luke 10:39-42, Matthew 8:14-16

READ — KEY QUESTION: What does this passage say?

REFLECT — KEY QUESTION: What does this passage mean?

RESPOND — KEY QUESTION: How should this change me?

What does this passage teach me about the character and nature of God?

How does this understanding of God change my view of myself?

What do I need to do to align myself with the revealed truth?

# DAY 5 — WOMEN WHO SERVED IN THE EARLY CHURCH
## Acts 9:36-41, Romans 16:12-15

READ — KEY QUESTION: What does this passage say?

REFLECT — KEY QUESTION: What does this passage mean?

RESPOND — KEY QUESTION: How should this change me?

What does this passage teach me about the character and nature of God?

How does this understanding of God change my view of myself?

What do I need to do to align myself with the revealed truth?

# FURTHER STUDY

Galatians 5:13-14

John 13:12-14

Philippians 2:1-11

James 2:14-17

giving

# GIVING

giving (v) — freely transfer the possession of (something) to (someone); freely devote, set aside, or sacrifice for a purpose.

As we begin this week's study, I want you to take some time to consider what is easy for you to give. Write down below a few things that come to mind.

Now, what do you find hard to give?

One of the most important lessons I've discovered about giving is this: It's easy for me to give what I have plenty of to people I care about. That is, I'm happy to give my daughter that shirt from my closet because I love her and I have a bajillion other shirts. But it's harder for me to give something I can't replace to someone I'm not close to.

We tend to give out of our abundance. And that's why we need to spend a week studying and praying about what giving really means.

Last week we focused on this truth: We serve for God's glory, not our own. This week, we will allow another truth to guide our study.

## God never asks us to give to Him what He hasn't already provided for us.

Stick with me, because I promise this is really good.

Last year, I led the ladies at my church through an exhaustive (and they might say exhausting) study of Exodus. We spent twenty-six weeks moving verse by verse through the account of God's deliverance of His people.

My favorite part to teach was the tabernacle. Not just because the tabernacle itself is a powerful image of God's desire to dwell with us, though that is a great truth. But I loved digging into what we discover about the offerings given to construct this beautiful structure.

Grab your Bible and look up Exodus 35:4-9 and 36:3-7. Read through those two passages.

Did anything stand out to you as you read? Write it down here.

Look with me at these verses:

Take up an offering among you for the Lord.
Let everyone whose heart is willing bring this
as the Lord's offering. (Exodus 35:5)

Meanwhile, the people continued to bring
freewill offerings morning after morning.
Then all the artisans who were doing all the
work for the sanctuary came one by one from
the work they were doing and said to Moses,
"The people are bringing more than is
needed for the construction of the work
the Lord commanded to be done."
(Exodus 36:3-5)

"Let everyone whose heart is willing." This was
a freewill offering. No one was required to
give.

"The people continued to bring ..." Every
morning the people brought more.

"The people are bringing more than is
needed." Stop here with me for a second. I'm a
pastor's wife, sister, daughter, granddaughter,
and great-granddaughter. I've been in church
almost every Sunday of my life. I've eaten
lunch with a pastor almost every Sunday of my
life. And I can assure of this—not one time
have I ever heard one say, "You know, I think
we can quit taking up the offering. We have
more than enough."

I think it's worth taking a few minutes to consider where this "more than enough" came from. Do you know?

Look up Exodus 12:35-36 and write down what happened.


So, where did the materials the Israelites needed to build the Tabernacle come from?


Remember that truth about giving? **God never asks us to give to Him what He hasn't already provided for us.**

The people were giving back to God what He had given them. And that is the heart of true giving.

We should respond eagerly to opportunities to give. And we can give generously of what we have been given.

Everything we have comes from God. When He calls us to obedience in this area, we can be certain He has provided all we need to follow His command.

GOD NEVER
ASKS US
TO GIVE
TO HIM
WHAT HE
HASN'T
ALREADY
PROVIDED
FOR US.

# DAY 1 — HOW TO GIVE
## Matthew 6:1-4

READ — KEY QUESTION: What does this passage say?

REFLECT — KEY QUESTION: What does this passage mean?

RESPOND — KEY QUESTION: How should this change me?

What does this passage teach me about the character and nature of God?

How does this understanding of God change my view of myself?

What do I need to do to align myself with the revealed truth?

# DAY 2 — CHEERFUL GIVING
## 2 Corinthians 9:6-15

READ — KEY QUESTION: What does this passage say?

REFLECT — KEY QUESTION: What does this passage mean?

RESPOND — KEY QUESTION: How should this change me?

What does this passage teach me about the character and nature of God?

How does this understanding of God change my view of myself?

What do I need to do to align myself with the revealed truth?

# DAY 3 — LEARNING CONTENTMENT
## Philippians 4:10-20

READ — KEY QUESTION: What does this passage say?

REFLECT — KEY QUESTION: What does this passage mean?

RESPOND — KEY QUESTION: How should this change me?

What does this passage teach me about the character and nature of God?

How does this understanding of God change my view of myself?

What do I need to do to align myself with the revealed truth?

# DAY 4 — WOMEN WHO GAVE IN THE GOSPELS
## Mark 12:41-44, Luke 8:1-3

READ — KEY QUESTION: What does this passage say?

REFLECT — KEY QUESTION: What does this passage mean?

RESPOND — KEY QUESTION: How should this change me?

What does this passage teach me about the character and nature of God?

How does this understanding of God change my view of myself?

What do I need to do to align myself with the revealed truth?

# DAY 5 — WOMEN WHO GAVE IN THE EARLY CHURCH
## Acts 16:14-15

READ — KEY QUESTION: What does this passage say?

REFLECT — KEY QUESTION: What does this passage mean?

RESPOND — KEY QUESTION: How should this change me?

What does this passage teach me about the character and nature of God?

How does this understanding of God change my view of myself?

What do I need to do to align myself with the revealed truth?

# FURTHER STUDY

1 Timothy 6:17-19

Luke 12:33-34

1 John 3:16-18

Galatians 6:6-10

# WORSHIPPING

worshipping (v) — show reverence and adoration for a deity; honor with religious rites.

Before we dig into this idea of worship, take a moment to read John 4:1-24. I'll wait here.

Familiar story, right? We'll look at it again this week. But for now, I want us to look specifically at one verse:

"God is spirit, and those who worship him must worship in Spirit and in truth." (v. 24)

Jesus is explaining to the Samaritan woman that she was asking the wrong question. Just a few verses before she said, "Our fathers worshiped on this mountain, but you Jews say that the place to worship is in Jerusalem" (v. 19). She was focused on WHERE to worship.

Look again at John 4:24:
"God is spirit, and those who worship him must worship in Spirit and in truth."

What two things does Jesus identify as necessary for worship?

If you're like me, you've heard those words countless times. But maybe you've never actually understood what it means to worship in spirit and in truth.

This simple sentence from Jesus reveals the two questions we should be asking when it comes to worship: WHO and WHAT.

<u>WHO should we worship?</u>
"God is Spirit," Jesus said. (John 4:24)

We worship God and God alone. This was the focus of the first four commandments given in Exodus. God alone is worthy of our worship.

When we focus on what we prefer instead of what pleases God, we elevate that which was created over the Creator.

We do this when we focus on HOW—the music, the environment, the instruments, the volume, the people around us, and a thousand other things.

Elevating the HOW over the WHO leads to worship centered on our preferences instead of God's pleasure.

<u>WHAT is the foundation of our worship?</u>
Not only can we place the how above the who in worship, we also elevate how over what.

When we allow our definition of worship to filter down to the songs sung before the sermon, we neglect the reality that our worship should be rooted in and inspired by the Word of God.

Do both our private and corporate experiences reflect the revealed truth of Scripture?

The Bible is the truth—the WHAT—that leads us into worship. Our focus should never be "What do I prefer?" The question we must consider is "What pleases God?"

When we look at Scripture, we discover time and again that styles and rituals are not what delight the heart of God. It is our hearts that matter most.

Greatest Act of Worship
In Romans, Paul explains the heart of worship.

Therefore, brothers and sisters, in view of the mercies of God, I urge you to present your bodies as a living sacrifice, holy and pleasing to God; this is your true worship. (Romans 12:1)

The greatest act of worship is not what we sing, it is how we live—offering our lives as living sacrifices is our "true worship."

Our worship should be pervasive, touching every aspect of our lives (see Colossians 3:17).

How we live should be evidence of our worship in Spirit and in truth.

As we think about our worship, these two questions should be our primary considerations:

WHO is my worship focused on pleasing?
WHAT guides my worship?

ELEVATING
THE HOW
OVER THE WHO
CREATES
WORSHIP
CENTERED
ON OUR
PREFERENCES
INSTEAD OF
GOD'S PLEASURE.

# DAY 1 — WORSHIP IN SPIRIT AND TRUTH
## John 4:21-24

READ — KEY QUESTION: What does this passage say?

REFLECT — KEY QUESTION: What does this passage mean?

RESPOND — KEY QUESTION: How should this change me?

What does this passage teach me about the character and nature of God?

How does this understanding of God change my view of myself?

What do I need to do to align myself with the revealed truth?

# DAY 2 — LIVING SACRIFICES
## Romans 12:1-2

READ — KEY QUESTION: What does this
passage say?

REFLECT — KEY QUESTION: What does this
passage mean?

RESPOND — KEY QUESTION: How should this change me?

What does this passage teach me about the character and nature of God?

How does this understanding of God change my view of myself?

What do I need to do to align myself with the revealed truth?

# DAY 3 — HEAVENLY WORSHIP
## Revelation 5:8-11

READ — KEY QUESTION: What does this
passage say?

REFLECT — KEY QUESTION: What does this
passage mean?

RESPOND — KEY QUESTION: How should this change me?

What does this passage teach me about the character and nature of God?

How does this understanding of God change my view of myself?

What do I need to do to align myself with the revealed truth?

# DAY 4 — WOMEN WHO WORSHIPED IN THE GOSPELS
## John 12:1-8, Luke 2:36-38

READ — KEY QUESTION: What does this passage say?

REFLECT — KEY QUESTION: What does this passage mean?

RESPOND — KEY QUESTION: How should this change me?

What does this passage teach me about the character and nature of God?

How does this understanding of God change my view of myself?

What do I need to do to align myself with the revealed truth?

# DAY 5 — WOMEN WHO WORSHIPED IN THE EARLY CHURCH
## Acts 1:12-14, 2:42-47

READ — KEY QUESTION: What does this passage say?

REFLECT — KEY QUESTION: What does this passage mean?

RESPOND — KEY QUESTION: How should this change me?

What does this passage teach me about the character and nature of God?

How does this understanding of God change my view of myself?

What do I need to do to align myself with the revealed truth?

# FURTHER STUDY

Isaiah 1:11-20

Acts 16:25-26

Romans 11:33-36

Ephesians 3:20-21

proclaiming

# PROCLAIMING

proclaiming (v) —declare something one considers important with due emphasis; give outward manifestation of something.

What does it mean to proclaim? This is one of those times when a good old dictionary comes in handy. Look the definition above and let's pay attention to two things.

Public declaration
Outward manifestation

Proclaiming involves speaking with others. It's giving emphasis to something we believe it important. And it's evident.

If we were to create an equation for what it means to proclaim it would look something like this:

## WHAT WE SAY + HOW WE LIVE = PROCLAIMING

In the Old Testament, God consistently and specifically called His people to look different. Peter wrote that we are to live as strangers and aliens in this world (1 Peter 2:10-12).

God says as His people we are set apart and called to holiness.

As image-bearers, we are to live in a manner that reflects His character.

Will we fail sometimes? Absolutely. But this is our calling, nonetheless. To move in this world as a reflection of the One who made this world.

How? Through the presence of the Holy Spirit and the transforming work of Scripture.

Our words and our actions must line up!

Proclaiming Jesus
Do you mind a quick dive into the Greek? The word used in Scripture for proclaim is *kerusso*.

*Kerusso* is a complementary word to *evangelion* (evangelize). We can evangelize about anything — from essential oils to our favorite football team. But this word for proclaiming is specific to "the public proclamation of the gospel and matters pertaining to it"[1]

*Kerusso* is used 61 times in the New Testament, 32 in the gospels and another nineteen times in Paul's letters with additional use in Acts, 1 Peter, and Revelation.

---

[1] Definition accessed on 11 February 2020
www.biblestudytools.com/lexicons/greek/nas/kerusso.html

You and I know the proclamation of the gospel of Jesus is a primary theme in the New Testament. This week's readings will help us uncover exactly what it means to proclaim and give us examples of what it looked like during Jesus' ministry and in the early church.

But before we move into our daily study, we need to look at one more question.

Who is called to proclaim?
Quick answer? All of us.

Let's quickly look at a few places in Scripture that lead us to this understanding.

Look up Genesis 1:27-28. What was God's instruction to Adam and Eve?



The first role assigned to us as image-bearers was physical multiplication—make more image-bearers. This is a shared calling, requiring both men and women to fulfill. We get that, of course.

Now, take a peek at Matthew 28:18-20. What is the command given here?

"Make disciples." Spiritual multiplication. This command is repeated in Acts 1:8.

But who is supposed to do this? In both of these passages we are only explicated told the disciples, all men, were present. Does that mean only men are responsible?

In order to answer that, let's head back into the Old Testament. Look up Joel 2:28-29. On whom does this text tell us the Spirit of God will come?

Now flip to Acts 2:16-21. This is part of Peter's great sermon on Pentecost. He quotes the verses from Joel.

God's Spirit has come to both men and women. And we are all called to proclaim the message of salvation through Jesus Christ.

There are many ways to do this and we will look at some examples this week. As you study this week, remember our equation:

WHAT WE SAY + HOW WE LIVE = PROCLAIMING

Let's be women whose words and lives are a testimony to the work of Christ in us!

# WHAT
## WE SAY
# +
## HOW WE
# LIVE
## =
# PROCLAIMING

# DAY 1 — COMMAND TO GO
## Matthew 28:16-29, Acts 1:8

READ — KEY QUESTION: What does this
passage say?

REFLECT — KEY QUESTION: What does this
passage mean?

RESPOND — KEY QUESTION: How should this change me?

What does this passage teach me about the character and nature of God?

How does this understanding of God change my view of myself?

What do I need to do to align myself with the revealed truth?

# DAY 2 — BE BOLD
## Romans 1:16-17

READ — KEY QUESTION: What does this passage say?

REFLECT — KEY QUESTION: What does this passage mean?

RESPOND — KEY QUESTION: How should this change me?

What does this passage teach me about the character and nature of God?

How does this understanding of God change my view of myself?

What do I need to do to align myself with the revealed truth?

# DAY 3 — AMBASSADORS FOR CHRIST
## 2 Corinthians 5:16-21

READ — KEY QUESTION: What does this passage say?

REFLECT — KEY QUESTION: What does this passage mean?

RESPOND — KEY QUESTION: How should this change me?

What does this passage teach me about the character and nature of God?

How does this understanding of God change my view of myself?

What do I need to do to align myself with the revealed truth?

# DAY 4 — WOMEN WHO PROCLAIMED IN THE GOSPELS
## John 4:28-30, 39-42, Mark 16:1-11

READ — KEY QUESTION: What does this passage say?

REFLECT — KEY QUESTION: What does this passage mean?

RESPOND — KEY QUESTION: How should this change me?

What does this passage teach me about the character and nature of God?

How does this understanding of God change my view of myself?

What do I need to do to align myself with the revealed truth?

# DAY 5 — WOMEN WHO PROCLAIMED IN THE EARLY CHURCH
## Acts 18:1-3, 24:26; 2 Timothy 1:5

READ — KEY QUESTION: What does this passage say?

REFLECT — KEY QUESTION: What does this passage mean?

RESPOND — KEY QUESTION: How should this change me?

What does this passage teach me about the character and nature of God?

How does this understanding of God change my view of myself?

What do I need to do to align myself with the revealed truth?

# FUTHER STUDY

Romans 1:16-17

2 Timothy 4:2-4

Hebrews 4:12

1 Peter 3:13-17

# FINAL THOUGHTS

I pray this study has both encouraged and challenged you to pursue a vibrant and flourishing faith! One of my favorite verses in Scripture is John 10:10

A thief comes only to steal and kill and destroy. I have come so that they may have life and have it in abundance.

Abundant life is God's design and desire for each of us. And, friend, I am on a relentless pursuit to know and live in that truth every day of my life. I hope you are as well.

I've been plotting and planning what I want to plant this year around Underwood Estates. There are some places I'd like to put some wildflowers and a fence I think needs some honeysuckle vine.

One thing I keep reminding myself is it takes time to get it done. Every year I'll add a little more and discover what will thrive.

The same is true for us spiritually. We will spend our whole lives growing. Keep sowing the seeds of faith in your life. Don't stop tending them or enjoying the blooms. And continue to look for ways to multiply!

# SCRIPTURE DIG

Scripture Dig is a multi-generational group for women who desire to study God's Word in community.

Scripture Dig is designed to encourage and equip women in the following stages:

- DEVELOP the habit of consistent time in the Word.
- IGNITE a passion for studying and helping others dig into Scripture.
- GROW in confidence in knowledge of the Bible and in understanding of God's character and nature.

Learn more and join our online studies at www.MyScriptureDig.com.

# ABOUT THE AUTHOR

As a Bible teacher and women's ministry speaker, Teri Lynne Underwood's greatest passion is encouraging and equipping women to dig into the riches we have in God's Word. She's been doing just that for over twenty years and prays for many more decades of investing in the women God places in her life.

She's the girl mom content manager for Million Praying Moms and has written two books specifically on the topic of prayer. *Prayers from the Pews: The Power of Praying for Your Church* is an invitation to pray with power and boldness for your church. *Praying for Girls: Asking God for the Things They Need Most* offers moms over 200 Scripture-based prayers covering five key areas of their daughters' lives. She has contributed to several books and wrote multiple devotions for the *(in)Courage Devotional Bible*.

All of those things pale in comparison to the joy she has as Scott's wife, Casiday's mom, and serving in her local church. You can find her most Wednesday nights, Bible in hand, either teaching a women's Bible study or sitting with a group of students digging into the Word.

Connect with Teri Lynne at
www.TeriLynneUnderwood.com.

Made in the USA
Middletown, DE
22 February 2020